REVISE BTEC

REVISION PLANNER

Planning your BTEC revision
A step-by-step guide

Series Consultant: Harry Smith
Introduction to mindfulness: Ashley Lodge

This Planner is for use with **BTEC Tech Award** (Level 1/Level 2), **BTEC Firsts** (Level 1/Level 2) and **BTEC Nationals** (Level 3) and can help with planning other external assessments you may take alongside these BTEC qualifications.

REVISE BTEC
STUDY SKILLS GUIDE

Also available:

Revise BTEC Study Skills Guide
978 1 292 33389 2

Full of tried-and-trusted hints and tips for how to learn most effectively, the **Revise BTEC Study Skills Guide** gives you techniques to help you achieve your best – throughout your BTEC studies and beyond!

For the full range of Pearson revision titles across KS2, 11+, KS3, GCSE, Functional Skills, BTEC and AS/A Level, visit:
www.pearsonschools.co.uk/revise

Published by Pearson Education Limited, 80 Strand, London, WC2R 0RL.
www.pearsonschoolsandfecolleges.co.uk

Text and original illustrations © Pearson Education Limited 2020
Typeset by QBS Learning Ltd
Illustrated by KJA Artists, John Hallett and QBS Learning Ltd
Cover illustration by Eoin Coveney

The right of Ashley Lodge to be identified as author of the mindfulness section of this work has been asserted by
him in accordance with the Copyright, Designs and Patents Act 1988.

First published 2020

23 22 21 20
10 9 8 7 6 5 4 3 2 1

British Library Cataloguing in Publication Data
A catalogue record for this book is available from the British Library

ISBN 978 1 292 33388 5

Acknowledgements
The publisher extends grateful thanks to Rob Bircher (author) and Dr Kathleen McMillan (consultant and co-author
of eleven titles in Pearson's bestselling 'Smarter Student' series and formerly Academic Skills Adviser and Senior
Lecturer, University of Dundee) for the Pearson *Revise GCSE Revision Planner* which has informed development of
the *Revise BTEC Revision Planner*. The publisher also extends grateful thanks to Brenda Baker, specialist reviewer
and contributor for the *Revise BTEC Revision Planner*.

Photo acknowledgements
Getty Images: Goodboy Picture Company/E+ 79, FreedomMaster/iStock 84, Peter Muller/Cultura 88,
Shutterstock: Africa Studio 81.

Notes from the publisher

1. While the publishers have made every attempt to ensure that advice on the qualification and its assessment is
accurate, the official specification and associated assessment guidance materials are the only authoritative source
of information and should always be referred to for definitive guidance.
Pearson examiners have not contributed to any sections in this resource relevant to examination papers for which
they have responsibility.

2. Pearson has robust editorial processes, including answer and fact checks, to ensure the accuracy of the content
in this publication, and every effort is made to ensure this publication is free of errors. We are, however, only human,
and occasionally errors do occur. Pearson is not liable for any misunderstandings that arise as a result of errors in
this publication, but it is our priority to ensure that the content is accurate. If you spot an error, please do contact
us at resourcescorrections@pearson.com so we can make sure it is corrected.

Contents

Your revision planner is also packed with **tips** and **strategies**, from setting up your revision space and using revision notes, to revision and memory techniques and ways to tackle questions.

About your revision planner

This planner helps you to **plan** and **track** your revision for your BTEC external assessments. It can also help you plan revision for external assessments you may take alongside BTEC. It helps you to be **organised** and **in control of your revision** using these steps:

☑ organise and chunk your revision time (pages 5–13)

☑ complete your revision wall chart (pages 14–15)

☑ plan and prioritise your revision topics using hit lists (pages 16–33)

☑ complete your revision planner and track your revision sessions (pages 34–75).

It also provides key ways to **prepare** for your assessments and introduces **mindfulness**, which can help keep you focused and calm.

> **Learner tip** I love my revision planner! It means I'm not missing anything or wasting time revising the same thing over and over again.

Features in your planner

 = work with your wall chart

 = work with the planner sections in this book

 = write something into this section

 = templates you can copy and use

 = check this with your teacher or tutor

 = reward yourself with a treat

Worked example
= an example of how to fill something in

Examiners' report
= guidance based on examiners' reports

Learner tip
= based on real learner experience

Mindfulness
= how mindfulness practice might help you – with audio

Understanding assessment types

Different assessment types have different requirements. Use the checklist below to identify the types you are taking. This can help when listing your assessments in **date order** on pages 7–8 and then when setting up your **revision wall chart**.

Your assessment types may include:

☐ **BTEC exam-style** (external assessment) – may be paper-based questions or onscreen

☐ **BTEC set tasks** (external assessment) – may be paper-based activities, onscreen or practical

☐ **BTEC tasks with pre-release** (external assessment) – may require you to carry out research and make notes, with supervised time, in advance of written or practical outcomes in exam conditions

☐ **BTEC assignments with completion dates** (internal assessment) – may be paper-based or onscreen and may include written, practical or work-based outcomes

☐ **other assessments** alongside BTEC: external or internal.

Understanding external and internal assessment

Externally assessed components/units	Internally assessed components/units
☑ Assessment takes place on externally set dates and times.	☑ Assessment takes place at key stages within the course.
☑ You may be assessed on anything you have studied.	☑ Assessment relates to specific criteria/learning aims.
☑ You put time aside to revise ahead of assessment.	☑ You put time aside in the course for each assessment.
☑ You use skills of memory, recall and application.	☑ You submit evidence by set dates within the course.

Planning for internal assessment

You may have completed your internal assessments when planning revision for your external assessments, or you may have some internal assessments to come. Here is an example plan – your details will be individual to you.

Internal assessment	Handout date	Submission date	Learning aims	Assessment type
Assignment brief 1	15/12	7/1	A, B	Case study
Assignment brief 2	30/3	18/4	C, D	Report
Assignment brief 3	28/4	12/5	E	Evaluation

Internal assessment checklist

This checklist can help with your internal assessment.

- ☐ Understand what you need for Pass, Merit or Distinction.
- ☐ Match the nature of the evidence you produce to meet the requirements of the assessment criteria/learning aims.
- ☐ Develop your study and research skills.
- ☐ Plan time to research evidence for assessments.
- ☐ Show that evidence is your own work and ideas.
- ☐ Acknowledge sources and do not plagiarise. Your work should not include copying from books or the internet.
- ☐ Manage your time so you hand in your evidence on time, meaning that resubmission is possible, if needed.

Internal assessments also help to prepare you for external assessments and good grades contribute to your overall BTEC grade.

Planning for external assessment

This Planner supports revision-planning for your **external assessments**. Start by listing your external assessments on pages 8–10, and also include any internal assessments you need to plan for in this period. The examples below may help you.

Worked example

Fill in the subject and details of each external assessment. This example is of a learner taking BTECs with GCSE Maths.

Subject, type, target grade	Unit / Component	Date, time and location	Remember to take...
Maths (External) Target grade: 4	Paper 2	4/6: 1.30 Main Hall	Calculator, pens, HB pencils, eraser, ruler, protractor, compasses

Check dates and details with your teacher or tutor. This example is of a learner taking a BTEC National in Sport.

Subject, type, target grade	Unit / Component	Date, time and location	Remember to take...
Sport (External task with pre-release) Target grade: Distinction	2 Fitness, Training and Programming for Health, Sport and Well-being	11/5: 9.30 Part A (1 week research, resource base) 18/5: 1.30: Part B, Main Hall	Research notes and black pens

Plan in any **internal assessments** within the revision period. You can use abbreviations such as LA for the learning aim. This example is of a learner taking a BTEC Tech Award in Digital Information Technology.

Subject, type, target grade	Unit / Component	Date, time and location	Remember to take...
Digital Information Technology (Internal) Target grade: Merit	2 Collecting, Presenting and Interpreting data	1/3 11am Rm 3 LA A: presentation 21/3 11am Rm 3 LA B: evidence 15/4 11am Rm 3 LA C: evidence	A Presentation notes B Dashboard C Written evaluation

Listing your assessment dates

Use this section (pages 8–10) to list the dates and details for your external assessments **in date order**. Include any internal assessments still to come within this revision period. Use pencil first. Check with your teachers or tutors so you have all the correct information you need.

Subject, type, target grade	Unit / Component	Date, time and location	Remember to take...

Subject, type, target grade	Unit / Component	Date, time and location	Remember to take...

Subject, type, target grade	Unit / Component	Date, time and location	Remember to take... COPY

Now note these dates on your **revision wall chart**. You could use red to make them stand out. The wall chart has 20 weeks and gives you an overview. You may not need all the weeks, or if more weeks are useful, you can make as many personal copies of the wall chart as you need.

Learner tip Start revising as early as you can! That way, if you find something difficult, you have time to work it out or find help.

Chunking your revision time

To help ensure quality revision, identify times for focused revision sessions. Plan more challenging revision for the times you are most alert. Start by describing a successful revision day so you can see how to chunk your time.

- When would your revision day start and finish?

....

- When would your best times for revision be?

....

- What times of day do you find it hardest to concentrate?

....

- If you need to revise/prepare with others, when would it be?

....

- How long would revision sessions and breaks be?

....

- When would you have meals?

....

- When would be the best time to build in exercise?

....

- How many hours of revision time do you have on most days?

....

Goals and rewards

Make sure you have **breaks** and **reward** yourself for achieving goals in each revision session. Note down:

 the **rewards** you will find motivating

 the **longer-term goals** your qualifications will help you achieve.

Working out your revision routine

Research shows that we focus better and feel more motivated when we **break tasks down into chunks.**

To make your revision time productive:

👍 revise for **20–25 minutes** with a **5-minute break**

👍 **vary** the topics you are revising.

Use your notes from page 11 and the example below to create your own revision routine.

Worked example

16.00–16.30: Relax/Snack

16.30–16.55: Maths – circle theorems

16.55–17.00: Break/Check phone

17.00–17.30: Health and Social Care – genetic inheritance

17.30–18.00: Meal

18.00–19.00: Homework/ Assignments

19.00: Relax/Reward

My revision routine

....
....
....
....
....
....
....
....
....

For each chunk of 20–25 minutes, create a revision cycle:

- **review the topic** (e.g. review notes, make a summary)

- **practise** (e.g. quiz yourself or try a question from the sample assessment material or a past paper)

- **review the answer** and make a note of what went well and what needs more work, and plan time to revisit and recap.

Working out revision time and priorities

Use the **four** steps below to work out your revision time for your **external assessments**. This will help when you complete your revision wall chart.

Worked example

Calculate **your** revision time here – this is individual to you   Example

			Example
1	Count up the number of days you have left between now and the start of your external assessments.		60 days
2	Decide how many hours you'll spend revising on an average day.		2.5 hours
3	Multiply the number of days you have by your revision hours per day to get your total revision hours.		60 days x 2.5 hours = 150 total
4	Divide your total revision hours by your total number of external assessments to get your average revision hours for each one.		150 hours ÷ 8 assessments = 18hrs 45m average each

Prioritising your revision time

You may need to give some subjects more revision time if:

- they are assessments you especially need to do well in
- they are subjects you find difficult – take into account your strengths and weaknesses as you plan your time
- they are subjects with more in them to revise
- you may need to revise some topics more than once.

Put a tick against any assessments on pages 8–10 that need more time. Adapt your plan to give them **extra time**.

13

Completing your revision wall chart

Use pages 14–15 to **complete** your **wall chart**. This gives you an **overview** of revision dates for your external assessments and key commitments.

You should **already** have filled in (see page 10):

• your external assessment dates

• your internal assessment dates in the revision period.

Now complete your wall chart. Use a pencil or erasable pen so you can adapt your plan if needed.

☐ Block out **other commitments** on your wall chart (e.g. activities and appointments), using a different colour.

☐ Block out time time to **prepare work** for any internal assessments in the revision period.

☐ Use the steps below to **complete the rest of your wall chart**. You could use different colours for different subjects. The examples opposite may help you.

1	To fill in dates for **each block of revision**, start with the earliest assessment date or one with extra hours.
2	Note the number of hours you have allocated to it (page 13).
3	Block out around half a day to revise for it on the day (or morning) before your assessment.
4	Take those hours away from the total time you have allocated to it.
5	Work backwards with your chart and allocate the rest of the time put aside for that assessment until the time is used up.
6	Do the same thing for all your assessments until your total revision time is used up.

Here are some examples of wall chart entries that might help you fill in your own wall chart.

Use abbreviations for subjects, and U for unit, C for component, P for paper, LA for learning aim.

Worked example

External assessments are in red   Other commitments are in green

Monday ☐	Tuesday ☐	Wednesday ☐	Thursday ☐	Friday ☐	Saturday ☐	Sunday ☐
HSC C3	Dentist 4pm	HSC C3	Tutorial	Biol P1 exam	Gym 10-11	DIT C3
HSC C2 LA2	HSC C3	assessment 10-12	10am Rm 4	9.15-11.00	Biol P2	Maths P1
Biol P1	Maths P1	School Hall	HSC C2 LA2	School Hall	Eng P1	
		Biol P1	Biol P1	Band 7pm		
		HSC C2 LA2		HSC C2 LA2		

Different subjects/components are in different colours (Tech Awards in Health and Social Care and Digital Information Technology; GCSEs in Biology, English and Maths)

Revision is blocked out for different subjects/units (BTEC National in Business; GCSE Maths)

Monday ☐	Tuesday ☐	Wednesday ☐	Thursday ☐	Friday ☐	Saturday ☐	Sunday ☐
Bus U10	Bus U6 Pt B	Bus U2	Maths P1	Bus U5 LA3	Film with	Swimming
LA2 hand in	onscreen	pre-release	Maths P1	Presentation	5am 6.30pm	10am
Maths P1	assessment	Pt A prep	assessment	2pm Rm 10	Bus U3	Bus U2 Pt A
Bus U6 Pt A	10am-1pm	Bus U5 LA3	2-3.30	Work exp	Maths P2	research
research	IT suite	Bus U3	School Hall	9.30-1pm		Bus U3
	Maths P1	Maths P1	Bus U5 LA3			Maths P2
	Bus U2		practice			
			presentation			
			Maths P2			

Internal assessment work is planned in

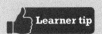
Learner tip Vary your revision chunks so you cover different subjects throughout the day.

Completing your revision hit lists

Use this section to plan your **topics** for each revision session.

- Topics are listed in the specification for your assessment, or in revision guides. Check with your teacher or tutor that you have the correct **topics** and any **options**.

- Complete the **Revision hit lists** in this section with your topics. There may be more pages than you need, or if further pages are useful you may make personal photocopies. Here are some different examples.

Worked example

List the topics you need to revise   Track your revision

Revision hit list: Subject: *Sport, Activity and Fitness*

Unit/Component: ....2........   Exam/Task: ....*Exam*........

TOPIC	Nearly there	Nailed it!
Components of fitness	☐	☐
Normative data tables to determine fitness status	☐	☐

Revision hit list: Subject: *English Language*

Unit/Component: ....1........   Exam/Task: ....*Exam*........

TOPIC	Nearly there	Nailed it!
Practise writing skills – letter writing	☐	☐
Prose fiction – identify and interpret themes and ideas	☐	☐

Revision hit list: Subject: *Health and Social Care*

Unit/Component: ....4........   Exam/Task: ....*Task*........

TOPIC	Nearly there	Nailed it!
Purposes and examples of research	☐	☐
Research issues: a) health conditions	☐	☐

Revision hit list: Subject: .... COPY

Unit/Component: .... Exam/Task: ....

TOPIC	Nearly there	Nailed it!
	☐	☐
	☐	☐
	☐	☐
	☐	☐
	☐	☐
	☐	☐
	☐	☐
	☐	☐
	☐	☐
	☐	☐
	☐	☐
	☐	☐
	☐	☐
	☐	☐
	☐	☐
	☐	☐
	☐	☐
	☐	☐
		☆

Revision hit list: Subject: .... COPY

Unit/Component: .... Exam/Task: ....

TOPIC	Nearly there	Nailed it!
	☐	☐
	☐	☐
	☐	☐
	☐	☐
	☐	☐
	☐	☐
	☐	☐
	☐	☐
	☐	☐
	☐	☐
	☐	☐
	☐	☐
	☐	☐
	☐	☐
	☐	☐
	☐	☐
	☐	☐
	☐	☐
		☆

Revision hit list: Subject: ....

Unit/Component: .... Exam/Task: ....

TOPIC	Nearly there	Nailed it!
	☐	☐
	☐	☐
	☐	☐
	☐	☐
	☐	☐
	☐	☐
	☐	☐
	☐	☐
	☐	☐
	☐	☐
	☐	☐
	☐	☐
	☐	☐

Your notes and class handouts are the backbone of your revision. Organise them into the right units/components and topics. Your revision hit list will help you to do this. Using a revision guide will also help you revise the relevant content, make focused notes and practise assessment-style questions.

Revision hit list: Subject: ....

Unit/Component: .... Exam/Task: ....

TOPIC	Nearly there	Nailed it!
	☐	☐
	☐	☐
	☐	☐
	☐	☐
	☐	☐
	☐	☐
	☐	☐
	☐	☐
	☐	☐
	☐	☐
	☐	☐
	☐	☐
	☐	☐
	☐	☐
	☐	☐
	☐	☐
	☐	☐
	☐	☐
		☆

Revision hit list: Subject:..

COPY

Unit/Component: .... Exam/Task: ....

TOPIC	Nearly there	Nailed it!
	☐	☐
	☐	☐
	☐	☐
	☐	☐
	☐	☐
	☐	☐
	☐	☐
	☐	☐
	☐	☐
	☐	☐
	☐	☐
	☐	☐
	☐	☐

Check your notes for any gaps. Make a list of any gaps and ensure you complete them. You could:

- check with your teacher or tutor
- cover them in a group revision session
- check a relevant textbook or revision guide
- share notes and quizzes with a revision partner.

Revision hit list: Subject: .... COPY

Unit/Component: .... Exam/Task: ....

TOPIC	Nearly there	Nailed it!
	☐	☐
	☐	☐
	☐	☐
	☐	☐
	☐	☐
	☐	☐
	☐	☐
	☐	☐
	☐	☐
	☐	☐
	☐	☐
	☐	☐
	☐	☐
	☐	☐
	☐	☐
	☐	☐
	☐	☐
	☐	☐
		☆

Revision hit list: Subject: .... COPY

Unit/Component: .... Exam/Task: ....

TOPIC	Nearly there	Nailed it!
	☐	☐
	☐	☐
	☐	☐
	☐	☐
	☐	☐
	☐	☐
	☐	☐
	☐	☐
	☐	☐
	☐	☐
	☐	☐
	☐	☐
	☐	☐

Learner tip Go through your notes and **condense** them:

- Be sure your notes are organised and you **understand** them.
- For each page, write a summary of the **main points**.
- Condense each summary down to **main ideas, key terms** and **key points**, with headings and bullets.
- Use your condensed notes as **revision cards** – to test yourself on the full content or to explain the summaries to others.

Revision hit list: Subject: ....

Unit/Component: .... Exam/Task: ....

TOPIC	Nearly there	Nailed it!
	☐	☐
	☐	☐
	☐	☐
	☐	☐
	☐	☐
	☐	☐
	☐	☐
	☐	☐
	☐	☐
	☐	☐
	☐	☐
	☐	☐
	☐	☐
	☐	☐
	☐	☐
	☐	☐
	☐	☐
	☐	☐
		☆

Revision hit list: Subject: ....

Unit/Component: .... Exam/Task: ....

COPY

TOPIC	Nearly there	Nailed it!
	☐	☐
	☐	☐
	☐	☐
	☐	☐
	☐	☐
	☐	☐
	☐	☐
	☐	☐
	☐	☐
	☐	☐
	☐	☐
	☐	☐
	☐	☐

Set up a tidy revision space so you can find all you need and are comfortable, quiet and can concentrate. You could work at home, in a library or in a public space. You may need to book access to specialist equipment or a larger space if required for performance, for example.

Revision hit list: Subject: ....

Unit/Component: .... Exam/Task: ....

COPY

TOPIC	Nearly there	Nailed it!
	☐	☐
	☐	☐
	☐	☐
	☐	☐
	☐	☐
	☐	☐
	☐	☐
	☐	☐
	☐	☐
	☐	☐
	☐	☐
	☐	☐
	☐	☐
	☐	☐
	☐	☐
	☐	☐
	☐	☐
	☐	☐
		☆

Revision hit list: Subject: .... COPY

Unit/Component: .... Exam/Task: ....

TOPIC	Nearly there	Nailed it!
	☐	☐
	☐	☐
	☐	☐
	☐	☐
	☐	☐
	☐	☐
	☐	☐
	☐	☐
	☐	☐
	☐	☐
	☐	☐
	☐	☐

Learner tip Make sure your revision space **works for you.** For example, make sure you have:

• access to the resources you need, such as books, pens, paper, internet, headphones, calculator
• good ventilation and no distractions (turn off your phone)
• water nearby, to keep hydrated
• a list of places and contact details to find help if needed.

Revision hit list: Subject: .... COPY

Unit/Component: .... Exam/Task: ....

TOPIC	Nearly there	Nailed it!
	☐	☐
	☐	☐
	☐	☐
	☐	☐
	☐	☐
	☐	☐
	☐	☐
	☐	☐
	☐	☐
	☐	☐
	☐	☐
	☐	☐
	☐	☐
	☐	☐
	☐	☐
	☐	☐
	☐	☐
	☐	☐
	☆	

Revision hit list: Subject: ....

Unit/Component: .... Exam/Task: ....

TOPIC	Nearly there	Nailed it!
	☐	☐
	☐	☐
	☐	☐
	☐	☐
	☐	☐
	☐	☐
	☐	☐
	☐	☐
	☐	☐
	☐	☐
	☐	☐
	☐	☐
	☐	☐

Learner tip It is important to be familiar with your assessments and what they require of you. Look at the **sample assessment material** and **mark scheme** for your external assessments. Your teacher or tutor can show you.

Revision hit list: Subject: .... COPY

Unit/Component: .... Exam/Task: ....

TOPIC	Nearly there	Nailed it!
	☐	☐
	☐	☐
	☐	☐
	☐	☐
	☐	☐
	☐	☐
	☐	☐
	☐	☐
	☐	☐
	☐	☐
	☐	☐
	☐	☐
	☐	☐
	☐	☐
	☐	☐
	☐	☐
	☐	☐
	☐	☐
		☆

Revision hit list: Subject: .... COPY

Unit/Component: .... Exam/Task: ....

TOPIC	Nearly there	Nailed it!
	☐	☐
	☐	☐
	☐	☐
	☐	☐
	☐	☐
	☐	☐
	☐	☐
	☐	☐
	☐	☐
	☐	☐
	☐	☐
	☐	☐
	☐	☐

Questions that require short answers may be recall types
of questions where you use your knowledge and memory
skills. They need less time. Often one mark can equal around
one minute. It can help your long-term memory if you build
in revision and recall sessions throughout your course,
recapping your knowledge.

Revision hit list: Subject: ....

Unit/Component: .... Exam/Task: ....

COPY

TOPIC	Nearly there	Nailed it!
	☐	☐
	☐	☐
	☐	☐
	☐	☐
	☐	☐
	☐	☐
	☐	☐
	☐	☐
	☐	☐
	☐	☐
	☐	☐
	☐	☐
	☐	☐
	☐	☐
	☐	☐
	☐	☐
	☐	☐
	☐	☐
		☆

Revision hit list: Subject: ....

Unit/Component: .... Exam/Task: ....

TOPIC	Nearly there	Nailed it!
	☐	☐
	☐	☐
	☐	☐
	☐	☐
	☐	☐
	☐	☐
	☐	☐
	☐	☐
	☐	☐
	☐	☐
	☐	☐
	☐	☐
	☐	☐

Questions that need longer answers often require you to apply your knowledge using skills such as analysis and evaluation. They may involve extended writing and are worth higher marks. Using words that link and signpost reasons can be useful, such as 'Another reason is...' or 'A different explanation is...' or 'However...'.

Planning your revision

Use this planning section to **plan** and **track** your **revision sessions**. You use the wall chart and planners differently.

Use the wall chart		Use the planner	
✓	for an overview	✓	to break revision sessions down
✓	to track your assessments	✓	to plan revision from your **hit lists**
✓	to track your blocked-out revision sessions	✓	to track the broken-down content in each revision session

Setting revision targets

Decide what you want to achieve in each session. This will motivate you and make your revision more effective. Look back at pages 11–13 on organising your revision time, and then work through your hit lists. Set revision session targets that are SMART: **s**pecific, **m**easurable, **a**chievable, **r**ealistic, **t**imely.

Your revision time

This planner section includes 20 weeks. There may be more weeks than you need or, if useful, you can make further personal copies. Check with your teachers or tutors so you have all the correct information you need about assessment dates in order to plan your revision sessions.

Learner tip Don't panic if you feel you've started late. You can still revise successfully. Prioritise and 'work smart'. Decide which assessments you need to do best in, and which parts need the most revision. Get into a routine and start each session with the high-priority material.

Completing your revision planners

Complete the **revision planners** in this section with your revision sessions. Here are some different examples.

Schedule your toughest subjects for when you are most focused, such as first thing in the morning, and remember to build in time to **revisit** and **recap** topics.

Worked example

If you plan a week at a time, you have flexibility from week to week. This extract of revision sessions includes recap, for Tech Awards and GCSEs.

Day	Session A	Session B	Session C	Session D	Session E	Rewards
Mon ☐	Maths P1: Recap adding fractions & revise subtracting fractions	Performing Arts C3: Meet with group to explore and agree theme	Performing Arts C3: Research Brecht techniques	Enterprise C3: Financial statement terminology	English P1: Recognise types of non-fiction texts	Music
Tue ☐	Maths P1: Converting fractions to percentages	Combined Science C1: Photosynthesis	Enterprise C3: Recap financial documents & revise payment methods		Geography P1: Climate change	Meet friends

You could use all the revision sessions or some of them. This extract of revision sessions includes recap, for a National in Engineering and an A Level.

Day	Session A	Session B	Session C	Session D	Session E	Rewards
Mon ☐	Maths: Quantities and units in the SI system; length	Engineering U1: Applying Newton's laws of motion	Engineering U1: Principles of conservation and momentum		Maths: Recap fundamental quantities and units in the SI system; time, mass	Gym
Tue ☐	Maths: Derived quantities and units; velocity; acceleration	Engineering U3: Manufacture process Characteristics and effects of metals		Engineering U3: Patents, registration, copyright & trademarks	Engineering U3: Regulatory constraints (legislation)	TV

Week beginning .... / .... with .... weeks to go

Day	Session A	Session B	Session C	Session D	Session E	Rewards
Mon ☐						
Tues ☐						
Wed ☐						
Thurs ☐						

Day	Session A	Session B	Session C	Session D	Session E	Rewards
Fri ☐						
Sat ☐						
Sun ☐						

Keep yourself motivated with a reward when you hit your revision targets.

Week beginning .... / .... with .... weeks to go

Day	Session A	Session B	Session C	Session D	Session E	Rewards
Mon ☐						
Tues ☐						
Wed ☐						
Thurs ☐						

Day	Session A	Session B	Session C	Session D	Session E	Rewards
Fri ☐						
Sat ☐						
Sun ☐						

A revision cycle of 20–30 minutes and revisiting the information helps you retain it in your long-term memory to recall it in your assessment. It keeps your brain alert and focused (see page 12).

Week beginning .... / .... with .... weeks to go

Day	Session A	Session B	Session C	Session D	Session E	Rewards
Mon ☐						
Tues ☐						
Wed ☐						
Thurs ☐						

Day	Session A	Session B	Session C	Session D	Session E	Rewards
Fri ☐						
Sat ☐						
Sun ☐						

These questions can help you review your revision sessions:

- What do I know or do that I didn't at the start of the session?
- How does what I've covered today link to what else I've covered in this subject?
- How would I summarise in five points what I've revised in this session?

Week beginning .... / .... with .... weeks to go

Day	Session A	Session B	Session C	Session D	Session E	Rewards
Mon ☐						
Tues ☐						
Wed ☐						
Thurs ☐						

COPY

Day	Session A	Session B	Session C	Session D	Session E	Rewards
Fri ☐						
Sat ☐						
Sun ☐						

These questions can help to direct your revision sessions:

- Based on what I've revised today, what do I think I should revise next?
- Thinking about the way that I revise, which strategies work best for me?
- Is there anything I can change about the way I revise to make it better?

Week beginning .... / .... with .... weeks to go

Day	Session A	Session B	Session C	Session D	Session E	Rewards
Mon ☐						
Tues ☐						
Wed ☐						
Thurs ☐						

Day	Session A	Session B	Session C	Session D	Session E	Rewards
Fri ☐						
Sat ☐						
Sun ☐						

Learner tip

Using **past papers** is a great way to revise for external assessments. Ask your teacher or tutor for information.

✓ Choose a time of day when your concentration is best.

✓ Use the **mark scheme** to check your answers.

✓ Note anything you need to revise further in a revision session.

Week beginning .... / .... with .... weeks to go

Day	Session A	Session B	Session C	Session D	Session E	Rewards
Mon ☐						
Tues ☐						
Wed ☐						
Thurs ☐						

Day	Session A	Session B	Session C	Session D	Session E	Rewards
Fri ☐						
Sat ☐						
Sun ☐						

COPY

Examiners' report

Read each question carefully so you **answer** the question you've **been asked.** The marks are a guide to the time you should spend on a question.

Week beginning .... / .... with .... weeks to go

Day	Session A	Session B	Session C	Session D	Session E	Rewards
Mon ☐						
Tues ☐						
Wed ☐						
Thurs ☐						

COPY

Day	Session A	Session B	Session C	Session D	Session E	Rewards
Fri ☐						
Sat ☐						
Sun ☐						

Examiners' report

You could use CUBE to help make sure you understand the questions:

- Circle the command word.
- Underline key information.
- Box key information in a case study or brief.
- Ensure you know what the question is asking of you.

Week beginning .... / .... with .... weeks to go

Day	Session A	Session B	Session C	Session D	Session E	Rewards
Mon ☐						
Tues ☐						
Wed ☐						
Thurs ☐						

Day	Session A	Session B	Session C	Session D	Session E	Rewards
Fri ☐						
Sat ☐						
Sun ☐						

COPY

Examiners' report

When answering a question:

⊘ Match your answer to the command word and what it requires of you.

⊘ If the question is set in a context, be specific and relate your answer to it, not just giving a general answer that could apply to anything.

⊘ Use subject-specific vocabulary to show your understanding.

Week beginning .... / .... with .... weeks to go

Day	Session A	Session B	Session C	Session D	Session E	Rewards
Mon ☐						
Tues ☐						
Wed ☐						
Thurs ☐						

Day	Session A	Session B	Session C	Session D	Session E	Rewards
Fri ☐						
Sat ☐						
Sun ☐						

Examiners' report

If you have a question with a context that involves data, show you can **apply** the data to the context. Do not just restate the data. For example, if drawing up a business plan, take into consideration data that showed losses in the last quarter.

Week beginning .... / .... with .... weeks to go

Day	Session A	Session B	Session C	Session D	Session E	Rewards
Mon ☐						
Tues ☐						
Wed ☐						
Thurs ☐						

Day	Session A	Session B	Session C	Session D	Session E	Rewards
Fri ☐						
Sat ☐						
Sun ☐						

Flow charts can help you to organise your notes. They are useful to show a sequence or cycle of events or processes, and the relationship between events. For example, with the digestive system:

Ingestion → Peristalsis → Digestion → Absorption → Egestion

Week beginning .... / .... with .... weeks to go

Day	Session A	Session B	Session C	Session D	Session E	Rewards
Mon ☐						
Tues ☐						
Wed ☐						
Thurs ☐						

Day	Session A	Session B	Session C	Session D	Session E	Rewards
Fri ☐						
Sat ☐						
Sun ☐						

Children's literacy activities

matching pictures — Visual discrimination

jigsaw puzzles

sound lotto — Auditory discrimination

nursery rhymes

Word recognition — labels — word snap

Decoding, segmenting and blending words

word-building cards   story books

Concept maps use a tree structure with many branches and clusters. They are useful to show links between the key ideas in a topic. They can help to develop ideas or arguments and to evaluate or compare. They can also illustrate reasons or causes.

57

Week beginning .... / .... with .... weeks to go

Day	Session A	Session B	Session C	Session D	Session E	Rewards
Mon ☐						
Tues ☐						
Wed ☐						
Thurs ☐						

Day	Session A	Session B	Session C	Session D	Session E	Rewards
Fri ☐						
Sat ☐						
Sun ☐						

Mnemonics are a useful memory technique where you use a word or phrase that is made from the first letter of key words. For example, PIES can stand for areas of human development: physical, intellectual, emotional, social.

Week beginning .... / .... with .... weeks to go

Day	Session A	Session B	Session C	Session D	Session E	Rewards
Mon ☐						
Tues ☐						
Wed ☐						
Thurs ☐						

Day	Session A	Session B	Session C	Session D	Session E	Rewards
Fri ☐						
Sat ☐						
Sun ☐						

Acronyms are a useful memory technique where you create a word made from the initials of key words. For example, BIDMAS can stand for: brackets, indices, division or multiplication, addition or subtraction.

61

Week beginning .... / .... with .... weeks to go

Day	Session A	Session B	Session C	Session D	Session E	Rewards
Mon ☐						
Tues ☐						
Wed ☐						
Thurs ☐						

Day	Session A	Session B	Session C	Session D	Session E	Rewards
Fri ☐						
Sat ☐						
Sun ☐						

Flash cards are a great technique for a quick quiz or for practice and recall. Place questions on one side of the card and answers on the other side.

REVISION PLANNER

Week beginning .... / .... with .... weeks to go

Day	Session A	Session B	Session C	Session D	Session E	Rewards
Mon ☐						
Tues ☐						
Wed ☐						
Thurs ☐						

Day	Session A	Session B	Session C	Session D	Session E	Rewards
Fri ☐						
Sat ☐						
Sun ☐						

Rhymes and songs or a catchy tune are techniques using sound to help you to remember key information. You could also use audio notes or podcasts to record your notes and listen back. Use meaningful file names so you can find them again.

Week beginning .... / .... with .... weeks to go

Day	Session A	Session B	Session C	Session D	Session E	Rewards
Mon ☐						
Tues ☐						
Wed ☐						
Thurs ☐						

Day	Session A	Session B	Session C	Session D	Session E	Rewards
Fri ☐						
Sat ☐						
Sun ☐						

Posters or sticky notes are useful visual techniques to summarise information and display diagrams – use colour and titles to create a logical structure.

Week beginning .... / .... with .... weeks to go

Day	Session A	Session B	Session C	Session D	Session E	Rewards
Mon ☐						
Tues ☐						
Wed ☐						
Thurs ☐						

Day	Session A	Session B	Session C	Session D	Session E	Rewards
Fri ☐						
Sat ☐						
Sun ☐						

COPY

Timelines are a useful visual technique to revise the order of things, and show causes and consequences. For example, life stages in childcare, and health and social care.

Years	0–2	3–8	9–18	19–45	46–65	65+
Stage	Infancy	Early childhood	Adolescence	Early adulthood	Middle adulthood	Later adulthood

Week beginning .... / .... with .... weeks to go

Day	Session A	Session B	Session C	Session D	Session E	Rewards
Mon ☐						
Tues ☐						
Wed ☐						
Thurs ☐						

Day	Session A	Session B	Session C	Session D	Session E	Rewards
Fri ☐						
Sat ☐						
Sun ☐						

Mind maps are a useful visual technique to show links between key ideas in a topic. They also show reasons and causes. They are great to help you evaluate and compare. Here is an example of a mindmap for Business Studies.

Methods
- audio
- visual
- written

Pitching ideas

The client

Responding to a commission

Purpose and audiences

Constraints
Scope

Funding
Budget
Relating to

Week beginning .... / .... with .... weeks to go

Day	Session A	Session B	Session C	Session D	Session E	Rewards
Mon ☐						
Tues ☐						
Wed ☐						
Thurs ☐						

COPY

Day	Session A	Session B	Session C	Session D	Session E	Rewards
Fri ☐						
Sat ☐						
Sun ☐						

A memory journey is a visual technique to help you remember things in order. Use a familiar journey or trip around your room. In your mind, stick each item to remember to a point on your route.

Week beginning .... / .... with .... weeks to go

Day	Session A	Session B	Session C	Session D	Session E	Rewards
Mon ☐						
Tues ☐						
Wed ☐						
Thurs ☐						

Day	Session A	Session B	Session C	Session D	Session E	Rewards
Fri ☐						
Sat ☐						
Sun ☐						

Keeping healthy helps you to concentrate.

- Eat well – at least five portions of fruit and vegetables a day.
- Keep hydrated – six to eight drinks of water a day.
- Exercise – 10 minutes will raise your heart rate and improve your mood.
- Sleep – helps you to remember, be creative and make decisions.

 Introducing mindfulness

The mindfulness practices in this planner can help you to stay calm and focused as you revise for assessments.

Important

If you feel that stress and anxiety are getting on top of you, speak to an adult who you trust. Opening up about how you feel can help during what can be an intense time.

If you have recently experienced the loss of a loved one, a traumatic event, have been diagnosed with mental illness, or have ongoing physical pain, it's really important that you check in with someone (such as a parent, teacher or tutor, counsellor or doctor) before doing these practices.

What is mindfulness?

Mindfulness is a great way to help you prepare for assessment. It is essentially about **awareness**. It trains you to notice **thoughts, feelings, sensations** and **what is happening** around you, without judging them. By doing this, you step away from automatic responses and observe what it means to be in the present with an open mind. This can help you to make better, more skilful decisions.

Training your brain

Your brain can be **rewired** to work in more **helpful** or **skilful ways**. In many ways it's like brain training. Just as people go to the gym and lift weights regularly to build muscle, so mindfulness helps train the brain when practised daily.

Brain training

Neuroscientists are starting to understand more about how mindfulness practice can help. Studies indicate that it helps in two main ways, especially when it comes to assessment.

1 It helps to increase the density in the front of your brain. This is the part associated with **memory**, and your ability to **solve problems** and **manage distraction**.

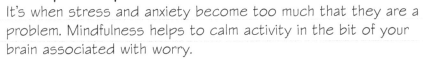

2 It helps you to manage strong or difficult emotions. Some stress and anxiety around assessment is natural and can **help boost performance**.
It's when stress and anxiety become too much that they are a problem. Mindfulness helps to calm activity in the bit of your brain associated with worry.

The form of mindfulness (Mindfulness-Based Cognitive Therapy) that we have used in this book was developed by three psychologists: Zindel Segal, Mark Williams and John Teasdale.

Connecting mind, body, emotions and behaviour

Mindfulness isn't just about training the mind – it's also about connecting with your body, emotions and behaviour.

- Emotions and feelings can affect your body and actions, and vice versa. Just as thinking can affect physical reactions (for example, feeling anxious can cause 'butterflies' in the tummy), so stress and tension in your body can affect your thinking.

- By becoming aware of your emotions, you can try to deal with them before they grow too strong or they start to take over your thinking.

Doing and being mode

It can be easy to want to get straight into doing a task like revision just to get it finished and out of the way. This is called **doing mode** – it helps you to gets things done, but may not help you to consider the **best way** of tackling the task.

Moving into being mode

Mindfulness helps by giving you a moment to pause and enter **being mode**. This allows time for you to:

* ground yourself and be fully focused on the present moment, so you experience things more fully

* take a calmer and wiser approach to a task, which will mean you're more effective.

The practices on pages 82–84 can help you create this mental space.

Being mode can help you think clearly

The pressures of revision and assessments mean you may avoid taking 'time out' for these practices. Yet regularly doing them so you can drop into 'being mode' can begin to give you greater mental space or clarity.

You can use the simple exercise on page 79 to help you come out of doing mode and move into being mode, creating a more mindful, moment-by-moment experience.

The purpose is to move away from doing things automatically. Instead, start to be fully in each moment and experience it more completely through all your senses. This will help give you clarity for your revision.

A mindful activity

You can practise mindfulness by applying it to an activity you do often, such as walking or eating. It's a great way to help keep yourself regularly in being mode. Here's a simple way you can bring mindfulness to making a drink.

- Take a moment to focus on your **breath**. Allow yourself to feel all the sensations in your body of the breath coming in and then passing back out. This helps take you out of doing mode and into **being mode**.

- What can you **hear**? For example, if making a drink, notice the sound of pouring the drink or boiling water.

- What can you **smell**? For example, if making tea, coffee or juice, notice how the smells **change** as you make it.

- What can you **see**? For example, notice the colours of a drink and how they **change**.

- What can you **feel**? For example, the warmth or coolness of a drink in your hands.

- What can you **taste**? For example, if taking a sip of drink, notice how it first tastes and any **changes**.

- Enjoy **being in the moment** as you carry out your chosen activity.

This simple exercise can have a big impact. Many people find they notice and experience far more.

- When you take time to slow down and live in a more moment-to-moment way, you are able to experience life more fully and appreciatively.

- This can then help to create a greater sense of calm.

Practising mindfulness

In addition to everyday mindfulness, you can do more formal practice, sometimes referred to as **meditation**.

Using the practice

As with any new skill, such as learning a new sport or instrument, mindfulness needs practice. Around 10 minutes of mindfulness practice a day can help you to move your awareness to be fully in the present moment in a non-judgemental way.

This can help you avoid the worry, anxiety and stress that can come from overthinking.

Practices in this planner

The three introductory practices on pages 82–84 are each accompanied by an audio file. They are useful techniques to help ground and anchor you in the present moment, encouraging you to be accepting and kind to yourself:

- Mindfulness of Breath and Body (around 10 minutes)

- The Body Scan (around 10 minutes)

- The Three-Step Breathing Space (around 3–4 minutes)

Being kind to yourself

Preparing for assessment can be stressful. It's important to take some regular time out to be kind to yourself, recharge your batteries, give your brain some breathing space, and acknowledge all the good work you're putting in.

Take regular breaks and enjoy some 'downtime' with your friends and family to help you recharge.

Using the three practices regularly will help keep you calm and focused during your revision period.

Mindfulness posture

Using a correct posture for mindfulness practice is really important. The three practices on pages 82–84 can be carried out in a seated position or lying down.

Sitting posture

Try to find a chair you can sit in that allows your feet to rest fully on the ground with your ankles, knees and hips all at right angles. Your back should be slightly away from the back of the chair so you can sit upright in an alert, but not tense, manner. Being comfortable will reduce distraction.

Mindfulness can help you take a healthy, effective approach to your revision.

Finding a space

Try to find somewhere you won't be disturbed. Switch your phone to silent or flight mode. Let the people you live with know that you'll be doing mindfulness practice so that they do not disturb you.

Mindfulness in schools

If you are in a school context and are interested in mindfulness, speak to your teacher or tutor. There may be a course in your school with a structured programme to follow, or you could search online for 'mindfulness in schools'.

 ## Practice 1: Mindfulness of Breath and Body

The **Mindfulness of Breath and Body** practice will help you to develop your **awareness** and **focus**. This can help as you revise and prepare for your assessments.

Focusing your attention

Our minds often like to wander. In this practice, you focus your attention on your **breathing** and on different parts of your **body**. It's a bit like shining a torch so you focus on just one thing at a time, feeling the sensations that arise.

Using this practice regularly will help your mind to wander less, leading to less worry and helping with concentration.

Developing your focus

It is normal for your mind to wander while meditating, as this is what minds do! Whenever your mind wanders, bring it back with a sense of kindness to focus on the breath or the body. Don't be frustrated, as it is just part of training your brain. This will increase your focus and train your attention each time. In addition:

- focusing on the body can help identify feelings in the body caused by stress, such as 'butterflies', tummy cramps, shaking hands, getting sweaty or your mouth going dry

- focusing on the breath can help with worry and stress around assessment, having a calming effect.

To access the audio file for Practice 1, please scan the QR code or visit http://activetea.ch/32wQnxo

 ## Practice 2: The Body Scan

Just as thoughts and emotions can affect our bodies, so stress and tension in the body can affect our thinking and our feelings. This practice will help to ground you and help you to sense more in your body. This can help you to move from thinking too much to becoming **calmer** in the revision process.

Grounding your body

Constant analysis of problems (such as worry around assessment) can be exhausting and may not help with a solution. **Sensing** what's going on in your body can help to reduce the time you spend analysing your problems. It **grounds you** back into your body, allowing you to see where you might be holding emotions and feelings as stress or tension in different parts of the body.

Developing your awareness

In the **Body Scan** practice, you move attention to different parts of the body, allowing you to feel where you might be holding emotions such as worry. As you hold each part of your body in your awareness, explore what feelings or sensations are arising in each one. This can help you to move away from thinking or analysing your problems too much. The practice can also improve posture, which can in turn improve thinking.

To access the audio file for Practice 2, please scan the QR code or visit http://activetea.ch/306mG4R

 **Mindfulness**

Practice 3: The Three-Step Breathing Space

Worrying about the past or future can distract you from what you are doing now. If you **focus on the present moment**, it is something you can change. This can help you to recharge to give you focus and help you think clearly with your revision and assessment.

Grounding in the present moment

The **Three-Step Breathing Space** practice helps you to ground yourself in the present and gives you moments to rest and recharge. It is structured a bit like an hourglass.

1 You do a 'weather check' of the mind, to **become aware** of what's going on. You observe your thoughts, for a more objective view of how busy or calm your mind is.

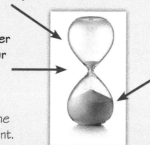

2 You then **gather** and **focus your attention** on your breath, helping to focus you in the present moment.

3 You then **expand** out that awareness to sensations in your body, becoming aware of where you may be holding emotions in the body as stress or tension.

Stepping back and recharging

This practice is useful if you start to feel stressed and want a pause to help you step back and get perspective. It is great as you can do it in three minutes or less and do it anywhere. Use it to recharge yourself while revising or to ground yourself before and around your assessment.

To access the audio file for Practice 3, please scan the QR code or visit http://activetea.ch/34EAMh4

Preparing for your assessment

It is important to be familiar with the **command words** used in your assessment, as they tell you what to do. Here are some examples of types you may commonly see.

Examples	Qualities of command word examples
Identify Which	• Often require a short answer • You use your knowledge to recall facts or features • Additional detail is usually not required
Describe Outline	• Require your understanding • You give a detailed account of something
Explain	• Requires your understanding • You make a point and then link it with detail to expand and explain the point
Discuss	• Requires clear understanding, applying knowledge to the context of the question • You make a balanced answer that considers all aspects of a topic and makes connections
Compare	• Requires your understanding, applying knowledge to the context of the question • You identify similarities and differences between things in a balanced way
Assess Analyse Evaluate	• Often require a longer answer, applying knowledge to the context of the question • You make a structured and balanced answer that may include different viewpoints, breaking things down and weighing up strengths and limitations • You may need to justify your points, where you support what you say to prove it is right or reasonable • A conclusion may be required

Command words for your assessments

Different assessments may use **different command words**. Check with your teacher or tutor to be sure you understand the ones used in **your** assessments.

Responding to questions

Assessments may involve scenarios, case studies or briefs with **realistic situations** and **contexts** so you apply your learning to real life. If these are **extended** with further information, consider the meaning of all the information you've been given and how it has developed.

Question	Show your ability to respond to information
Short answer questions	☑ Read the context carefully each time. ☑ Relate your answer to the context given to you. ☑ Apply your learning and theories to real-life situations.
Longer answer questions	☑ Analyse and interpret the given context in relation to your learning and how theory applies. ☑ If data is involved, don't just restate it – apply it in context. ☑ Plan and write detailed answers that link to the context.
Questions that involve a process	☑ Ensure you fully understand what is required of you in the process (for example in designing a technological solution, a performance, a presentation or piece of art and design). ☑ Break down your response into achievable parts. ☑ Focus on each stage, evaluate it and keep on track.

Extended writing

Questions worth higher marks often involve **extended writing** where you need to explain your thinking. Make sure you:

☑ keep your answer **relevant** and refer back to the question

☑ use **specialist** terms to show your subject knowledge

☑ use **paragraphs** to give your answer a clear structure

☑ **connect** your points to show clear, logical understanding. Words that link (because, due to, therefore) can be useful.

Examiners' report

Techniques can help you, for example, PEEL: Point: make one point. Explain the point. Evidence: justify the point and explanation. Link back to the question.

Top assessment tips

This checklist is based on learners who did well in their assessments.

- [ ] Bring together your own **personal checklist** of things to revise and do, to achieve good grades. Your teachers or tutors will be glad to help you.

- [ ] Start your revision **as early as possible**. You need time to **revise** the topics, check you **understand and remember** them, and **revisit** them.

- [ ] Get lots of **past papers**. Work through them and use the mark schemes to see what you got right and what you need to revise to do better. Know your strengths and target your weaknesses.

- [ ] If you have an onscreen assessment, make sure you are **familiar** with how it works and how to use it.

- [ ] If you've got big assessments that you're revising for early, **also** build in time for later assessments – you need to revise for them, too.

- [ ] The Easter holidays can be prime revision time. Use your time **wisely** to get serious about revision.

- [ ] Get plenty of **sleep** the night before an assessment.

 Learner tip Get **creative!** Revise in ways that work for you. I put sticky notes with key words on them all round the house so everywhere I went, I could be revising.

Access arrangements

If you need access arrangements for assessments, such as scribes or readers, make plans with your teacher or tutor in advance.

Assessment day checklist

1 Know **when** and **where** your assessment takes place. Arrive **at least 15 minutes** early, allowing for delays. Make sure you are hydrated and comfortable.

2 Check you have the **equipment** you need. For a **written assessment**, you need **black pens**. Check with your teacher or tutor if anything else is needed. If you are allowed a **calculator** it may need to meet specific requirements.

3 If your assessment is a **task with pre-release**, make sure your preparation is fresh in your mind. If allowed notes in the assessment, make sure you have them ready.

4 If your assessment is **practical**, make sure you have prepared, practised and have everything ready. If you are part of a group, make sure your roles are clear.

5 Be ready to **keep track of time** and allocate time according to the number of marks for each question. Check your answers if you have time.

Learner tip **Think positively.** You've worked hard and can be proud of how you've prepared. Take some deep breaths to help you relax and ground you in the moment.

On **Results Day**, if you go in person you can discuss plans. If sharing results, remember you are all different, with plans that are individual to each of you.

We wish you success with your assessments and your future plans!